MW01290276

Homemade Dog Treat Recipes

How to Make Organic and Natural Dog Treats for Your Best Friend

Table of Contents

Introduction

Homemade dog treats are very healthy and easy to make. Contrary to what most people think, making organic and natural dog treats is not about making tasteless food. If you love your dog, then it is important that you make sure that the food that he or she is eating is safe and nutritious. The problem with giving your dogs store-bought treats is that you don't know whether they contain ingredients that are unhealthy for dogs. For instance, the FDA has issued warnings to consumers about several chicken jerky products that were associated to kidney failures in dogs so if you love your dogs, give him doggie treats that come with homemade goodness. After all, homemade dog treat recipes always spell love in every bite. This book will share great homemade dog treats that you can give your canine family members.

Chapter 1: Homemade Dog Treat Recipes

Make your own cookie treats for your dog with these wonderful and simple recipes that you can make in your home. Be sure to make large batches of these recipes because your dog will surely gobble up every nib of these sweet treats. You can give these cookie treats to dogs as reward for their good behavior or after training them.

Cinnamon Doggie Bun Bites

This tasty doggie bun bites has cinnamon that is very good for the dog's health. This is a treat that dogs will surely love.

Ingredients:
¼ cup finely chopped walnuts
1 teaspoon cinnamon
2 tablespoon honey
1 large egg
¼ cup canola oil
½ cup water or milk
¼ teaspoon salt
1 teaspoon baking powder
2 cups whole wheat flour

Directions:

1.) In a bowl, combine the flour, salt and baking powder and mix well.
2.) In a separate bowl, mix together water, oil and egg and lightly beat the mixture.
3.) Gradually add the wet ingredients to the flour mixture and blend well to form a soft dough.
4.) Roll the dough on a floured surface and knead for a minute.
5.) Make buns out of the dough and sprinkle the buns with honey, cinnamon and nuts.
6.) Bake for 15 minutes or until the bun turns golden brown.

Homemade Mutloaf

This healthy doggie meatloaf recipe is loaded with lean meats and nutritious vegetables to make your dog active as well as maintain his or her healthy weight.

Ingredients:
1 tablespoon olive oil
2 cloves garlic
¼ cup chopped zucchini
¼ cup chopped spinach
¼ cup chopped carrot
½ cup wheat germ
2 whole egg
½ cup cottage cheese
1 ½ lb ground chicken
1 ½ cups chicken broth
½ cup amaranth

Directions:

1.) Add chicken broth and amaranth in a sauce pan and bring the mixture to a boil.
2.) Reduce the heat and simmer for another 20 minutes. Set aside and let it cool.
3.) Preheat the oven to 350^0 Fahrenheit.
4.) In a large mixing bowl, mix the eggs, meat, cottage cheese and vegetables.
5.) Add the wheat germ and the cooled amaranth and olive oil.

6.) Put the mixture to a loaf pan and bake for one hour or until a done.

Note: If you cannot find amaranth, you can substitute it for barley.

Ice Paws Treat

This icy dog treat is made from yogurt and tuna which is something that your dog will surely like to nibble during a hot summer day.

Ingredients:
2 teaspoon garlic powder
1 small can tuna in water
2 cartons of plain vanilla

Directions:

1.) Mix all of the ingredients in a bowl thoroughly.
2.) Put the mixture on ice trays and freeze overnight.
3.) Serve cold.

Healthful Pumpkin Balls

This healthy pumpkin snack is not only delicious but it is also filled with fiber, beta-carotene, potassium and iron that your dog needs in order to be healthy.

Ingredients:
1 teaspoon cinnamon
¼ teaspoon baking powder
¼ teaspoon baking soda
2 cups whole wheat flour
2 tablespoon vegetable oil
4 tablespoon water
4 tablespoon molasses
½ cup mashed pumpkin

Directions:

1.) Preheat the oven to 350^0 Fahrenheit.
2.) In a bowl, mix together vegetable oil, molasses and water.
3.) Add the rest of the dry ingredients and mix well to form a soft dough.
4.) Scoop a spoonful of the dough and roll into balls using your hands.
5.) Set the balls on a cookie sheet and flatten with a fork.
6.) Bake for 25 minutes or until the dough turns golden.

Apple Crunch Pupcakes

If your dog loves sweet treats, then this fruity apple crunch pupcakes will definitely make him enjoy his doggie treats.

Ingredients:
1 tablespoon baking powder
1 cup dried apple chips
4 cups whole wheat flour
1 medium egg
1/8 tablespoon vanilla extract
2 tablespoon honey
¼ cup unsweetened applesauce
2 ¾ cups water

Directions:

1.) Preheat the oven to 350^0 Fahrenheit.
2.) In a bowl, mix together the applesauce, water, egg, honey and vanilla. Mix well.
3.) Add the remaining ingredients and blend well to form a smooth batter.
4.) Pour the batter to muffin pans lined with cupcake liners
5.) Bake for 45 minutes.

Fishy Dog Treats

Different dogs have different preferences when it comes to the food that they want to eat. If your dog loves to eat fish, then this homemade dog treat is for you. You can substitute tuna with sardines.

Ingredients:
Finely grated parmesan cheese
190 grams whole wheat flour
2 eggs
2 small tuna (drained)

Directions:

1.) Preheat the oven to 350^0 Fahrenheit.
2.) Mash the fish in a bowl using a food processor and add in the eggs and flour to achieve the fluffy sponge cake mix.
3.) Spoon the mixture to the baking tray and sprinkle lightly with parmesan cheese.
4.) Bake for 5 minutes until the edges shrink away from the sides of the muffin pan.

Doggie Trail Mix

Trail mix isn't only enjoyed by humans. Combine leftover grains from your fridge to create a delicious trail mix. It is best enjoyed if you take your dog at the park.

Ingredients:
Dried fruits (no raisins or grapes)
Vegetables (zucchini, carrots and peas)
Potatoes
Pieces of leftover meat (rinse off any flavoring)

Directions:

1.) Cut all ingredients to ½ inch thick pieces.
2.) Mix everything in a bowl and place everything in a food dehydrator until dry.

Frozen Peanut Butter and Yogurt Treats

This is a perfect snack to cool down your dog during the summer of after a playful session.

Ingredients:
1 cup peanut butter
32 oz plain yogurt

Directions:

1.) Melt the peanut butter in a microwave oven.
2.) Once melted, pour the yogurt to the bowl and mix everything together.
3.) Pour the mixture onto cupcake papers.
4.) Place in the fridge to solidify.

Sweet Kiss Cookies

This homemade dog treat is made from ingredients that your dog will surely like. It also comes with parsley which is high in Vitamins C and A. Moreover, parsley can also help maintain proper digestion and keeps his or her breath sweet-smelling at all times thus the name.

Ingredients:
1 cup peanut butter
½ cup non-fat dairy milk
½ cup water
2 large eggs
1 tablespoon dried parsley flakes
1 cup rolled oats
2 cups whole wheat flour

Directions:

1.) Preheat the oven to 300^0 Fahrenheit.
2.) Mix all of the dry ingredients in a large bowl.
3.) In a separate bowl, beat the eggs and add the water and peanut butter. Mix well to incorporate the wet ingredients.
4.) Combine the dry and wet ingredients.
5.) Mix well and make sure to remove all clumps.
6.) Knead the dough with your hands.
7.) Take a rolling pin and flatten the dough on a leveled surface.

8.) Use a cookie cutter and cut out cute bone shapes on the dough.
9.) Bake for 30 minutes or until the cookies turn golden brown.
10.) Let it cool to harden before feeding the treat to your dog.

Homemade Milk Bone

Dogs love munching on milk bones. This healthy milk bone doggie treat will surely make your dog happy to get his reward.

Ingredients:
1 egg
½ cup powdered milk
1/3 cup unsalted butter
¾ cup chicken broth
3 cups whole wheat flour

Directions:

1.) Preheat the oven to 350⁰ Fahrenheit.
2.) Mix the wet ingredients well and set aside. Do the same thing with the dry ingredients.
3.) Combine both wet and dry ingredients to create a smooth dough.
4.) Knead the dough for two minutes and roll onto a floured surface to 1/4 inch thickness.
5.) Cut dog bone shapes on the dough and place them on a baking sheet lined with parchment paper.
6.) Bake for 40 minutes or until brown.
7.) Let the cookies cook before feeding to your dog.

Peanut Butter Oven Treats

Peanut butter is a healthy food to feed your dog. It is a good source of protein and vitamins and minerals. There are many homemade dog treat recipes that use peanut butter as the main ingredient including this healthy peanut butter oven treats.

Ingredients:
1 ¼ cups hot water
1/3 cup peanut butter
1 cup rolled oats
2 cups whole wheat flour

Directions:

1.) Preheat the oven to 350^0 Fahrenheit.
2.) In a mixing bowl, combine all ingredients and mix well to form a dough.
3.) Knead the dough on a flat working surface.
4.) Use a roller pin to flatten the dough and cut out the desired shapes that you want.
5.) Place the cookies on a baking pan lined with parchment paper. Do not use cooking spray as it is unhealthy for your dog.
6.) Bake in the oven for 30 minutes or until golden brown.

Pink Delight Cookies

They say dogs are colorblind but because of their amazing sense of smell, they will be able to sniff the rainbow goodness of this simple pink delight cookies recipe. When making these cookies, make sure that you do not use artificial coloring as food dyes are very dangerous for dogs.

Ingredients:
½ cup sugar-free strawberry jam
½ cup water
½ cup low sodium chicken broth
½ cup peanut butter
2 tsp cinnamon
½ cup rolled oats
2 cups whole wheat flour

Directions:

1.) Whisk together the oats, cinnamon and flour in a mixing bowl.
2.) In a separate bowl, mix the peanut butter, flour, strawberry jam and chicken broth and microwave for 15 seconds.
3.) Pour the wet ingredients to the dry ingredients gradually. Mix well using a fork until a soft dough forms.
4.) Scoop rounded balls of the dough and place them on a baking sheet lined with parchment paper.

5.) Bake at 325^0 Fahrenheit in a preheated oven
for 15 minutes or until golden.

Note: The strawberry jam gives the cookies its pink
color. If you do not have any strawberry jam, you can
omit this ingredient and proceed to making the
dough. You can also substitute with other berries
including pitted blueberries.

Beef Jerky

This beef jerky recipe is a great way to keep your dog busy. It is also a great way to train him or her not to chew on your things. Below is a great organic and natural dog treat that you can give to your canine friend.

Ingredients:
1 cup beef liver
1 lb ground beef

Directions:

1.) Chopped the liver into tiny pieces and mix them to the ground meat.
2.) Scoop the meat and place it in a jerky gun to form jerky sheets. If you don't have a jerky gun, you can flatten the meat before placing them in the dehydrator.
3.) Set the dehydrator to 165^0 Fahrenheit for three to four hours until the meat has become crunchy.

Chicken Doggie Biscuits

Chicken is a good source of lean protein. Use this homemade dog treat recipe to create delicious biscuit nibbles for your dogs.

Ingredients:
1 cup cornmeal
2 cups whole wheat flour
3 eggs, lightly beaten
3 tablespoon coconut oil
½ cup chicken broth
1 lb chicken meat, ground

Directions:

1.) In a saucepan, bring to a boil the water and ground chicken.
2.) Place the mixture in the blender. Add the eggs and olive oil and blend together until the mixture become incorporated.
3.) Pour the mixture in a mixing bowl and add the flour and cornmeal.
4.) Drop spoonfuls of the mixture on cookie sheets that are lined with parchment paper.
5.) Bake for 20 minutes in a 450^0 Fahrenheit preheated oven.
6.) Let the biscuits cool before giving to your dog.

Chapter 2: Special Homemade Dog Treat Recipes

Special homemade dog treats are great food to give to senior dogs because they are easily digested and do not give any stomach problems to your dogs. Moreover, these treats are also beneficial for dogs who suffer from special medical conditions. However, these recipes are not only restricted to old dogs. You can use them for puppies that are still learning to feed themselves. Below are the different soft organic and natural dog treats that you can prepare for your dogs.

Pumpkin Puree Perfection

Pumpkin is very nutritious for dogs and they are loaded with vitamins E and C as well as other antioxidants. Moreover, the high fiber content in pumpkin is also great in maintaining healthy weight for your dogs. The beta carotene that pumpkin contains is also good in reducing cataract and heart problems in your dogs.

Ingredients:
½ cup powdered milk
¾ cup cream of wheat, uncooked
15 oz pumpkin, pureed

Directions:

1.) In a mixing bowl, combine all the ingredients and mix well.
2.) Place the ingredients on a baking pan.
3.) Bake in a 300^0 Fahrenheit oven for 15 minutes.
4.) Let it cool before serving to your dog.

Apple Cinnamon Biscuits

Cinnamon and apples are great foods for dogs that are suffering from arthritis and gout. It is a high fiber food that comes with a lot of vitamins and minerals so your senior dog can still get the nutrients that it needs to stay healthy at his or her age.

Ingredients:
2 large organic eggs
½ cup powdered milk (can be substituted with cream of wheat)
5 cups brown rice flour
½ cup olive oil
1 cup cold water
1 tablespoon parsley
1 teaspoon cinnamon
1 cup organic applesauce

Directions:

1.) Mix all the ingredients together until clumps are no longer formed.
2.) Knead the dough on a flat working surface.
3.) Roll the dough and cover with a plastic wrap.
4.) Refrigerate the dough for 1.5 hours or overnight.
5.) Flatten the dough using a rolling pin and cut out the desired shape the next day.
6.) Bake for 30 minutes in a 350^0 Fahrenheit oven or until golden brown.

7.) Let it cool until it hardens.

Vegetarian Doggie Muffins

If your dog does not like to eat his or her veggies, then this vegetarian doggie treat will make your pup eat vegetables. This treat is a great way to add more nutritional value to what your dog eats. It is also a great treat to give to dogs that suffer from obesity.

Ingredients:
¾ cup whole wheat flour
¼ cup dry oats
1 cup flax seed
¼ cup water
¼ cup molasses (plus 2 tablespoons more if needed)
2 cups shredded carrots
1 cored, seeded and chopped apples

Directions:

1.) Combine all ingredients in a bowl.
2.) Lightly butter the muffin pans and place enough batter on the muffin pans.
3.) Bake for 15 minutes at 400^0 Fahrenheit preheated oven or until golden brown.
4.) Let it cool before giving your dog a treat.

Doggie Veggie Treat

This doggie veggie treat is a great source of vitamins and minerals for your dog. It is low in fat as well as phosphorus thus great for dogs that have restricted diet requirements and also those suffering from obesity.

Ingredients:
½ cups cold water
6 tablespoons low sodium vegetable broth
1 teaspoon dried parsley
1 cup cooked vegetables
2 ½ cups rice flour (can be substituted with brown rice flour)

Directions:

1.) In a large mixing bowl, combine all dry ingredients and mix well. Set aside.
2.) In a separate bowl, mix the wet ingredients and gradually add them to the dry ingredients.
3.) Remove all clumps from the dough.
4.) Knead the dough on a flat surface and cut out desired shapes.
5.) Place the treats on a baking sheet lined with parchment paper.
6.) Bake for 25 minutes in a 350^0 Fahrenheit preheated oven.

Pumpkin Doggie Bites

This doggie treat is made from pumpkin which is a good source of beta carotene and fiber. It is a great doggie treat to give dogs that have weight problems.

Ingredients:
1 teaspoon allspice
2 teaspoon baking powder
2 tablespoon rapeseed oil
4 tablespoon water
4 tablespoon smooth peanut butter
80 grams rolled oats
120 grams pumpkin, cooked and mashed
190 grams whole meal flour

Directions:

1.) Preheat the oven to 350^0 Fahrenheit.
2.) In a large mixing bowl, combine the oats, flour, allspice and baking powder.
3.) In another bowl, combine the oil, peanut butter and pumpkin and mix well until smooth.
4.) Add all the ingredients together to incorporate everything.
5.) Turn the dough on a floured surface and knead for a minute until the dough no longer becomes sticky.
6.) Roll out the dough and cut mini shapes with your favorite cookie cutter.

7.) Bake for 12 minutes then turn off the oven. Leave the cookies inside the oven for another 30 minutes.

8.) Let the cookies cool before feeding to your dog.

Veggie Bagels

This veggie bagel recipe is loaded with a lot of vegetables that are good sources of fibers, vitamins and minerals. You can give your dogs the bagels as they or you can slather it with a good amount of peanut butter to make it more delicious.

Ingredients:
½ cup carrots, chopped
½ cup spinach, chopped
¼ teaspoon baking powder
1 egg
¼ teaspoon baking soda
1 teaspoon vegetable oil
½ cup wheat flour
2 ½ cups white flour
¾ cup water

Directions:

1.) Combine all the dry ingredients in a mixing bowl.
2.) On a separate bowl, add the dry ingredients. Mix until all of the ingredients are well blended.
3.) Gradually add the wet ingredients to the dry ingredients and mix.
4.) Shape small round balls of dough and poke holes in the middle of the dough.

5.) Place the bagel balls in a preheated oven and cook for forty five minutes at 300^0 Fahrenheit.

Peanut Butter and Banana Doggie Biscuits

There are many special homemade dog treat recipes that you can try and one of them is this special vegan doggie diet. This particular recipe is great for senior dogs that are suffering from kidney and liver diseases. It is a low fat treat that still has the same goodness as other rich doggie treats out there.

Ingredients:
½ teaspoon cinnamon
1 ¼ cup whole wheat flour
½ cup applesauce
1 cup oats
½ cup peanut butter
1 mashed banana

Directions:

1.) In a mixing bowl, mix all of the ingredients together to form a soft dough.
2.) Knead the dough on a flat surface for several minutes.
3.) Let it cool before flattening using a rolling pin.
4.) Cut out the desired shapes of the doggie biscuits.
5.) Place the doggie biscuits on a baking sheet lined with parchment paper.
6.) Bake in a 350^0 Fahrenheit preheated oven for 15 minutes or until the edges become golden.

7.) Let the cookies cool before storing them in the fridge.

Pureed Liver and Carrots

This pureed dog treat is great for senior dogs. It is a good source of iron, beta carotene and vitamins and minerals. Since it is already pureed, it does not overwork the stomach of old dogs thus they don't get any indigestion with this treat.

Ingredients:
1 lb liver, chopped
1/3 cup grated carrots
1 egg
1 ½ whole wheat flour
1 cup corn meal
1 teaspoon oregano

Directions:

1.) Mix together the wheat flour, corn meal and oregano.
2.) Add the rest of the ingredients to the flour mixture and mix well.
3.) Spoon the batter into a pan lined with parchment paper and bake for 30 minutes at a 350^0 Fahrenheit preheated oven.
4.) Once it has cooled, cut the pureed liver and vegetables into squares.

Sweet Potato Biscuits

This sweet potato dog biscuit is not only naturally sweet but it is also rich in fiber, potassium and antioxidants that can improve the overall health of your dog.

Ingredients:
1 egg, lightly beaten
1 ¾ cup whole wheat flour (can be substituted with brown rice flour)
1 cup sweet potato, mashed

Directions:

1.) Preheat the oven to 350^0 Fahrenheit.
2.) Mix all ingredients in a large bowl to form a soft dough.
3.) Roll the dough to small balls and place them on a cookie sheet lined with parchment paper.
4.) Press the dough so that the biscuits are ¼ inch thick.
5.) Bake until golden brown and let them cool on a wire rack.

Spinach Treat

This is a healthy treat that you can give to your dog. This is especially true if you want your dog to lose weight.

Ingredients:
½ teaspoon baking powder
2 ½ cups whole wheat flour
½ cup applesauce, unsweetened
¼ cup plain yogurt
¾ cup mixed vegetables (cauliflower, broccoli and carrots)
1 cup fresh baby spinach

Directions:

1.) Preheat the oven to 350^0 Fahrenheit.
2.) Dice the spinach and the mixed vegetables in a food processor.
3.) Put the diced vegetables on a large bowl.
4.) Add the yogurt and applesauce to the veggie mixture.
5.) In a medium bowl, blend together the baking powder and flour.
6.) Mix the ingredients together to form the dough.
7.) Knead the dough until a firm ball is achieved
8.) Flatten the dough with a rolling pin and cut into shapes with a cookie cutter.

9.) Place the cookies on a baking sheet lined with parchment paper.

10.) On a separate bowl, mix yogurt and water.

11.) Lightly brush the cookie dough with the yogurt mixture.

12.) Bake in the oven for 20 minutes.

13.) Let it cool before feeding your dog.

Homemade Liver Brownies

Dogs do suffer from anemia too and these homemade liver brownies. This liver brownie is a good source of Vitamin A and protein which are both good for your dog's health.

Ingredients:
½ cup dried parsley
2 ½ teaspoon granulated garlic
2 eggs
2 cups wheat germ
2 cups corn meal
2 lb chicken liver

Directions:

1.) Put the liver inside t food processor and add the other ingredients to create a smooth texture.
2.) Spread the liver mixture on a cookie sheet lined with parchment paper.
3.) Bake for 350⁰ Fahrenheit for about 35 minutes.
4.) Let it cool and cut into squares.
5.) Place inside a zip lock bag and store inside the refrigerator.

Low Fat Spinach Doggie Balls

If your dog is extra pudgy, then this low fat spinach doggie balls is a great snack to keep your dog's weight in check.

Ingredients:
1 teaspoon dried oregano
2 tablespoon grated Parmesan cheese
¾ cup rolled oats
¾ cup whole wheat flour
1 tablespoon olive oil
1 cup chopped spinach

Directions:

1.) Preheat the oven to 350^0 Fahrenheit.
2.) Mix together spinach and olive oils in a bowl.
3.) In a separate bowl, mix together the flour, cheese, oats and oregano.
4.) Make a well at the center of the flour mixture and add the spinach.
5.) Stir until it forms a soft dough.
6.) Knead the dough on a floured surface and flatten it using a rolling pin.
7.) Use a cookie scooper and make rounded balls and place them on a baking sheet lined with parchment paper.
8.) Bake in the oven for 30 minutes or until golden brown.

Apple Carrot Treats

These apple carrot dog munchies are rich in fiber and beta-carotene. It is a great doggie snack for dogs that love sweet treats. It is a great snack for dogs that suffer from obesity.

Ingredients:
½ cup unsweetened applesauce
1 egg
1 cup grated carrots
1 cup brown rice flour

Directions:

1.) Preheat the oven to 350⁰ Fahrenheit.
2.) In a bowl, mix all the ingredients to form a dough.
3.) Roll the dough using a rolling pin and make small balls using your hands.
4.) Place the small dough on a cookie sheet lined with parchment paper.
5.) Flatten the dough using a fork.
6.) Bake for 15 minutes or until golden brown.

Chapter 3: Tips and Tricks in Making Homemade Dog Food Treats

If you are one of the many pet parents who are concerned about the types of foods that your dog eats, then it is important that you make your own homemade dog treat recipes. The recipes included in this book are very healthy for your dogs. This chapter will focus on the tips and a trick on making organic and natural dog treats.

Things to Consider When Making Doggie Treats

If you are planning to make dog treats, you might not get a good reaction from your dog the first time you feed them with your homemade recipes. The thing is that dogs are like humans too and they can be discriminate about the types of foods that they eat. Below are the things that you need to consider when making doggie treats that your dog will surely eat.

Ingredients

The ingredients play a vital role in the overall taste of the doggie treats. It is crucial that you pick ingredients that are natural and organic. This is because dogs are allergic to many types of foods. If your dog is allergic to one of the ingredients that you are using, then you can always substitute for healthier options. For instance, if your dog is allergic to gluten or wheat, you can substitute wheat flour to rice flour, amaranth flour, quinoa flour, millet or corn starch.

Preference

If your dog is also very picky about the kinds of food that it eats, then make sure that you make dog foods that he or she will likely eat. For instance, if your dog has a sweet tooth, then make doggie treats that are also sweet but only use natural sources of sugar such as honey and applesauce. Never put white sugar or artificial sweeteners on your homemade dog treats.

Calories

Pay attention to the number of calories that your dog is getting from your doggie treats. As much as possible, do not overfeed your dog with treats. The thing is that obesity is a condition that largely affects many breeds of dogs. Only feed several pieces of treats each day to your dog.

Texture

Texture is very important in making dog treats. If your dog is not suffering from old age, you need to feed him with hard treats because it can make his teeth strong. Moreover, giving hard doggie treats also help eliminate the buildup of plaque.

Size

The best treats are those that can be taken in a single bite. The best thing about giving small-sized homemade dog treats is that you make sure that they are not eating too much calories.

Storage

It is also important that you store your dog treats the same way you would store cookies intended for people. Keep it in a cool, dry and dark place for cookies or biscuits. If you prepare soft foods like muffins or purees, make sure that you store them inside the fridge. If stored properly, your organic and natural dog treats can last for up to two weeks in a cool environment or 2 months inside the fridge.

Don'ts for Baking Doggie Snacks

Baking homemade dog treat recipes is fun but what if it is your first time baking for your dog, then it is important that you know about the top don'ts in baking doggie snacks. Below are the things that you should never do when baking homemade dog treats.

- **Do not pick a hard recipe:** Never pick a hard recipe if you have never even experienced baking anymore. Fortunately, all recipes included in this book are very easy to follow so they are very easy even if you are a first time baker.

- **Do not use ingredients that your dog will not like:** As the pet owner, it is important that you understand what your dog likes and does not like to eat. Start making dog treats using ingredients that your dog likes.

- **Do not use ingredients that your pet is allergic to:** There are many dogs that allergic to wheat and if your dog is one of them, then substitute ingredients to something that your dog has no allergic reaction to.

- **Don't put all ingredients inside the bowl:** Follow the guide when making homemade dog treat recipes. Do not just put all the ingredients in one bowl. If you dump everything together, your dog treats will not turn out good as indicated in the recipe.

- **Do not expect for your homemade treats to last longer than store-bought ones:** Store-bought doggie treats are laden with preservatives so even if you store them out in the open, they can still last for a long time. Unfortunately, homemade dog treats can go moldy after a week if stored at room temperature. Make sure that you make just enough batches that can last for a week otherwise you will be throwing the leftovers away.

- **Do not feed your dogs all snacks in one sitting:** Your homemade treats might be healthy but it is still not a good idea to feed your dogs all of the treats in one sitting. His treats should comprise 10% of his diet. Feed only three or four small portions of the doggie treats to your dog. This is just enough to keep your dog happy.

Conclusion

Feeding your dog with delicious doggie treats need not be expensive. You can make your own dog treats right at the comforts of your home. Not only will your dogs love them but you also guarantee that the ingredients used in making healthy doggie treats are safe and has high nutritional value to give your canine family members good overall health.

The ideas, concepts, and opinions expressed in this book are intended to be used for educational and reference purposes only. Author and publisher claim no responsibility to any person or entity for any liability, loss, or damage caused or alleged to be caused directly or indirectly as a result of the use, application, or interpretation of the material in this book.

44208146R00031

Made in the USA
San Bernardino, CA
09 January 2017